THE ACT OF CARING: A SELF-HELP GUIDE TO SIMPLE SELLING

****

BUILDING RELATIONSHIPS TO GROW AND "EXCEL" IN SALES

MICHELLE WOLFORD

The Act of Caring: A Self Help Guide to Simple Selling

Building Relationships to Grow and "Excel" in Sales

For information about publishing or book creation services, contact Co-Pilot Publishing LLC at

Copilotpublisher@gmail.com

Printed on acid-free paper

Library of Congress Control No:

ISBN: 9798882536441

Co-Pilot Publishing LLC, 2024

About the Cover Designer and Graphic Design Artist:

Lauren Milligan

Lauren Milligan has been a Graphic Designer for 6 years. She graduated with an Associate of Arts Degree from Northeast Community College. She will graduate from the University of Nebraska - Lincoln with a Bachelor's Degree in Advertising and Public Relations and a Minor in Communications.

The Act of Caring: A Self-Help Guide to Simple Selling

****

Building Relationships to Grow and "Excel" in Sales

The Act of Caring, skillfully written by Michelle Wolford, applies not only to selling but to living. To Michelle, the concept is simple - care about others first to make sales. The personal anecdotes make it an easy read, written with humor and heartfelt emotion that leaves one inspired and encouraged.   This guide is for everyone who wants to improve both their personal and business relationships.

-Susan Gieschen

"Michelle finds a way to capture methods to increase your sales through building relationships. This self-help guide is a quick and easy read with tactics that are easy to employ. Let yourself be immersed in Michelle's methods, especially if you are new to sales. You cannot go wrong with this one!"

-Bethany Childers
BSBA, MSOL, SHRM-SCP, PHR

"Michelle's ability to pack basic sales skills and knowledge into an easy, fun read is outstanding. She has the ability to draw you in and make you smile through her writing. This book should serve as a basic guide for any new salesperson."

-Donielle Smith
Life Liberator Coach & Multi-Million Dollar Income Earner with LegalShield

TABLE OF CONTENTS

PROLOGUE

At what point in life is enough, enough?

I have asked myself that so many times. Wondering, when will I know enough to write it all down? When will I know enough to "write a book?"

Well, I think it's time. I have been in sales for more than 25 years now. I have done some amazing things, and I've done some not so great things.

As many of you may know...Sales is not always peaches and cream!

I started when I was probably 11 or 12 years old trying to sell myself as a babysitter. I then moved to McDonald's thinking this was a big step in the right direction. Phhht!

Well, I shouldn't say it didn't help, because it did. It taught me how rude people can be. How *not* to act.

A couple years later, I worked as a Professional Fencer. Not the kind that stabs you with fancy swords, either. We are talking the sweat and tears kind of fencing, out on the ranch in the hot sun with sweat pouring off my body, fencing.

After nearly slicing my leg in half (for those of you that know…you know). A roll of red-barbed wire came cruising down my leg! That was a trip to the ER!

Next up, was a call center to sell credit cards. Boy was this a deal! I refer later in my book to the "No! No! No! approach." You'll see why this is a gem, in due time.

I did work at Armstrong's Bait & Tackle. It was the best job I ever had, in my whole life. Just Ivan and myself, working and stocking a bait and tackle shop. This was a dream come true. Unfortunately, it was just a summer gig, and the Armstrong's sold to a man that did not see the world the same as Ivan and I had.

I was yelled at for counting worms incorrectly, so you know the saying, "All good things must come to an end?" Well, this too shall pass.

Let's see. What did I do next in life. Oh, yes! I went to college. I was a State Champion Triple Jumper. I missed the All-State Gold Medal by a ½ inch. Dang! But anyway, it is a proud moment that I will never forget. So, I digress.

My whole point to this rambling is that I quit a time or three. I quit because I cared too much, some may say.

I cared so much that I searched my entire life for something fulfilling; something that would change me forever. I had found it in Fire & EMS, but that would soon be taken from me too.

I broke my neck lifting a 300+lb patient out of the back of the ambulance when the X-Frame Stretcher's legs came crashing to the ground.

I couldn't catch a break in life. You'll see why I say this, and stand by it, as you read more in this book.

Sales is one of those things in life that can be bittersweet. One moment, you are making money like a wild woman, and the next, you are broke and almost on the street. At least that's how I felt in the earlier years of my career.

As I sifted through the best years of my life, I worked from call centers, all the way up to being an Account Executive for one of the largest companies in the entire United States of America. In fact, I sold one of the largest accounts the company had ever laid its eyes on.

But, why didn't I stay? Operations were horrible, and my mission in life was to care for others. I could not bear to sell something when I knew the service was not top-notch.

That leads me to where I am today. I've bounced all over the grid trying to find success. Well, ladies and gentleman. I think I may have finally found my home.

After 20 some years of ups and downs, who would have ever thought that I would land where I have landed, in insurance! What!?

It's been a wild ride, but in all seriousness, I have found a person that cared enough about people to inspire me to help others in the same way that I have always wanted to help other people. An entrepreneur who got it. A philanthropist who sees life the same way I do. An inspiration who saw something in me.

I can't thank this woman enough for opening my eyes to the world around me. A world that was constantly taking from me. A world that I never dreamed would ever give back. A world that most people find captivating, but yet a world that still takes from us day after day.

Have I been a super success at this? Not yet. Will I make a career out of insurance? I'm not sure. What I do know, is that I have found a role model. An inspiration worth seeing where this goes. An opportunity has presented itself where I can share the *care* that I once hoped to share through a world where pain and suffering was all I knew.

You see, I was a Critical Care Paramedic, Firefighter and Rescue Diver. I worked Fire & EMS for 19 years (the years I can officially count). My dad was a Fire Chief, Paramedic, and Dive Rescue Captain.

I used to ride on the cow catcher to put out smaller grass fires when I was knee-high to a grasshopper. I also sat passenger on many, many car accidents. I even ran on the drag team most of my life, starting when I was little. I've seen my fair share of distress. Maybe this is why I think caring is so important.

I say this all to share with you the why behind me. The why that stood behind me surfing the world, searching, while others just found a paycheck. The why that makes me, well, me. The act of caring.

Why do you care that I care?

Such a simple concept, yet no one seems to be able to master it. Why?

Let me try to explain... It is intuition to never trust anyone until you get to know them. Hence the adage, we work only with those people that we "know, like and trust." - Bob Burg.

Does this really make sense though? I know people that seem to trust me minutes after I speak with them. There are others that never trust me and I've known them for life. Could it be that we are all just "wired differently?"

I ponder this point from time to time and conclude that every person in this entire universe is different. I find myself wondering, is this even a question that can be answered?

I believe everyone can answer this question in their own mind and live toward a vision of truth that they, and only they, have the power to design.

"What if?" – Chris Felton. What if I could understand what you were thinking? What if I could meet your every need the second that we met? What if I could project your future? What if I could satisfy your wants? That would just be too easy in a world that is hard and complex. So, let's get back to reality.

What do most people want when they approach me at the office? They want to receive. A man I once knew asked me, "What is better? To give or to receive?" It was a question I hadn't thought much about. But Gary Barnes made it clear that you have to receive before you can give. You see, receiving creates the appreciation for the WHY in giving.

I "give" for the feeling that I receive in exchange, but if I never receive, I never experience that "feeling" that creates the true meaning behind "giving." Interesting, isn't it?

Why do you care that *I* care? Because, it is engrained in our brains. We are human. It is called emotion. Some are born with more than others. Some may experience things that make them less emotional at times. Some may never have the ability to show emotion, but that is a whole different novel. And then there is me, who is super emotional all the time and very sensitive to the world around me. Emotional intelligence is an amazing piece of life. We should value it more deeply.

What is it about *you*?

People make me have questions. Why?

Because I am a people pleaser. In my line of work, that is what we do. Day in and day out, we try to please people and satisfy their needs. This is called "Sales."

Sales is an interesting creature. Every new prospect that I meet, whether it be over the phone or in-office, poses a new set of questions. What is it about *you*?

What brings you in today? What is the reason for your call? How can I help you? I hear these questions all the time and wonder why we keep answering the same. I need this. I need that. What if someone simply said, "I want to receive what you are going to sell me." That just sounded weird, didn't it? Back to my prior point, though. You have to be willing to receive or this will never work. Am I correct?

Anyway, my whole point was to get you to think outside the box. Do we really listen to people when we are asking questions, or are we just following protocol?

Some days, I get it. We sink into that "just getting through the day" mode. But really, if you want to be successful in your career, what is it that you need to do? You need to ask meaningful questions and LISTEN for meaningful responses.

I mean, don't think this doesn't go both ways! You can be an excellent listener and have someone who isn't a good communicator. And vice versa. You can be an excellent communicator and not have a good listener. My point is, finding a meaningful relationship with someone you want to do business with is invaluable.

Heed caution when you look to "work with someone." I value every single person who comes through our doors. I value every single person who cares enough to call. My mom used to always say, "Remember the golden rule. Treat others as you wish to be treated." If we could all hold that same respect with one another, wouldn't this world be a better place?

What is it about *me*?

People just "like" me.

Personality seems to be everything. Can we do well in sales if we don't have the greatest personality? I would say, "yes." I've known a person or two that I wondered how they got to where they were going, but they apparently had a different operating system than I do.

I'm far from being perfect, but I do know how people work. I pride myself in a simple understanding of thought. I am blessed with an ability to read a person pretty quickly and react to their body language.

I also have the ability to mirror. No, I'm not being weird. It's something that I have a natural ability to do. Mirroring, in my opinion, allows me to get to your level and in a hurry. I tend to mimic the behavior of the person I am working with. This matches their persona and takes me into their world for the moment I am working with them. It works.

My development in the sales world has trained my brain to react to others in ways that some people have never thought about.

Does this make me special? No. When I think about how I work with people, I am grateful for all the years of education that led me to this point. I took college courses for a total of 16 years, but I'm not here to brag about me. My point, again, is that I am thankful for all that life has thrown at me and for all the bullets I have dodged to get me to a point where I think like I do.

Is "selling" just another word, or is it deeper?

"Selling" is a word. But, is it just that?

I say the word "selling" is much deeper. It is a relationship that is super complex and can be especially meaningful. When I am "selling" someone, I am building a life-long relationship with them. That's my goal, at least, and I wish the impact of this word meant so much more to so many more people. This world would be a better place.

I find myself asking why people like to "sell"? Guess what the most popular answer is (in my opinion)? Because I can make good money. BOO!!! That is a terrible, horrible, pathetic reason to "sell" to someone! It makes me nauseated to think that the reason over half this world is "selling" to others is because of what they are receiving MONETARILY.

There is that word again. "Receive." Is it okay to receive from your sales? Of course, it is! However, what if more than half of the world is "receiving" the wrong message! When I "sell", I "receive" a feeling that I was trusted, that this person cared enough about me to give me private information about them. They trusted me with their safety. They trusted that I will be there in the future when questions arise. They trusted that I will not betray them.

Yes, I receive monetary reward, but that is the last, LAST thing on my mind. Some may think this is silly, but I feel this is what sets me apart.

If I shift my focus to the person I am "selling" to and make that transaction solely about them satisfying their needs and building that trust, don't you see more value than a focus on how big my paycheck may be if I just make this sale?

Let that soak in for a few minutes...

We all like money. It's what makes the world go round. I love money. BUT the impact we can make on someone's life in a

simple transaction is worth its weight in gold.
Literally. All the money in the world cannot
make you feel the way trusted relationships
can make you feel, especially when you
multiply them day after day after day. You
become someone special. Someone *you* can
know, like and trust.

To the point or too blunt?

Many say I am too blunt. Am I?

I like to think I just think more than others, and words tend to fall out of my mouth. Now, don't get me wrong. I am not good at popping off with witty and quick comebacks. I'm definitely a slower processor. Give me time to write it down though, and look out! I can out-think most, if you give me time.

Back to sales. To the point or too blunt? What am I talking about? The sale. The big close.

How many of you have been asked if you are a closer? Sometimes this determines if you get a job or not. And I say "job" because people looking to place folks in careers know better than to ask for just a "closer." There are many more qualities necessary to be an excellent sales' person.

Closing the sale is a delicate thing. People want to be "sold" but they do not want to be "SOLD." When I get to the point in a business relationship that I feel it is time to close, I simply say, "How are you feeling? Should we get this done?" Hopefully, by this point, I have built a solid foundation and am at a place where this is a given. Usually, I get their payment information and we get the deal done. Does it always work? No. But it is a successful way to approach a sale.

My close rate is very good. I won't share exact statistics because it changes every day. I do know that my inspiration (my boss) "pays me for my value, not my time." -Gary Barnes. That is everything to me, so it means more than receiving just a dollar amount. To be appreciated and valued. There is nothing greater.

The Never-Ending Story...

The Never-Ending Story in my life is a book I am building of successes that I have worked hard to obtain. It's a book of people who I have cared for and stuck my neck out for.

These folks are the reason for my existence. Without them, I'd have no meaning or purpose. Some people think work is just work. But should it be that way? I wish everyone could have a career. Jobs are just jobs. *Careers* change lives. They impact us. Another of my favorite words: IMPACT.

When I think of the word impact, I get excited! I want to impact as many people as I can.

The Old "NO! NO! NO!" Philosophy

Sell them until they say "NO" three times! WHAT!!!???

Are you "selling" or are you "SELLING!"? Holy cow! What in the world got into someone's mind when they came up with this. Let's just beat the person into submission. Wow. Just wow.

I am not a fan of this technique, clearly. I don't mean to discredit anyone. It can be a successful way to build a book of business. I like to think of this as a hard-covered book. I like my books to be more of a soft-cover, not that it's easy to destroy, but that it's not stiff and cold in its approach. A soft-covered book of business was built on a solid, warm and caring foundation.

This is badgering someone to the point that they say "yes" just to get you off the phone or out of their presence. I do not like this. It seems demoralizing. It is very cold and non-relational. Enough said? Okay, let's move on.

My "Take" – for Realz!

I "take" it that Sales is not meant to be a "bully thing." I "take" it that when you close a deal, you are not "closing" a relationship. I "take" it that people like me because I "show them how much I care."

HAMMER DOWN!

Get after it! You must be persistent!

Persistence is a key in sales. I cannot emphasize this enough!

My inspiration likes to use the word "consistency." It, to me, is interchangeable with my word "persistence." Both words follow the path of least resistance. This path leads straight to success, as long as you don't falter. You must be consistent and persistent every single day and with every single client, every single time.

I wear a bracelet on my wrist with words of encouragement. The bracelet I have on at the moment says "PERSISTENCE." My best friend, Jason, gave me this as a reminder to fuel myself toward success.

I keep a pipeline of the folks I work with on a daily basis. Every single day, I make sure to update my pipeline and my notes to myself about the interactions I have with every customer I touch that day. I use colors to keep track of "maybe next times" and "in the green" customers. I use red for the "hard stops." Black is for the "never call me again" scenarios—the "Do Not Call" requests.

This is a simple system, but one that helps with separation. One that defines things for me. It follows the rules of our society. Green means go. Yellow is to proceed with caution. Red means stop. Black rarely comes into the picture, but defines those that choose to never be contacted again, as explained above. I, then, use blue to define closed deals. Blue represents success! Blue is the company color. This, obviously, can be changed to match your company's color.

This system is not for everyone, but it certainly helps me with my personal accountability. It's a quick visualization of the work being performed. At one quick scroll and glance, I can see that blue is a mass of sales that have closed, while green is new business opportunities.

Let's talk about the yellow and red.
Yellow is an opportunity that just lies down
the road at some point. It is when someone
tells me to reach out in 6 months or a year, or
more. I put them ALL on my calendar with a
contact name and phone number to follow up.
Follow up is very important.

The red is really what I want to focus
on. RED DOES NOT MEAN "DEAD END."
People have changes in their lives. They may
have been mad when they told you to never
call them again. They may have been going
through the loss of a family member and had
been up all night when you called them to try
to "sell" them. They may have been in the
best mood they have ever been in and told
you yes, to call them tomorrow and now it's a
bad, bad day. You just never know.

My point is that life changes from day to
day. We don't know what someone else is
thinking or going through from one moment
to the next. Think with your heart, not with

your cold thoughts. This is critical—demonstrating empathy.

Red simply shows that during that contact, you did not have a favorable response. It is okay to reach out again at some point. These "leads" as we call them, are what I call challenges. Challenges are fun. I make a point of revisiting my leads the following year.

Why a year later? They may have forgotten you, but if you made good notes and bring up something memorable, they may be able to recall you. This subconsciously creates a connection. People like to feel connected. Do you see where I am going with this? Boom, you have a connection. You have been around a while which builds a feeling of trust and loyalty. Voila! We have a new opportunity for a sale!

Ask Questions – Discovery (Leave No Stone Unturned)

I have had a few notable inspirations in my life.

Dylan was one of my favorites. He was my Sales Manager at Deep Rock Water (DS Services of America) in Denver, Colorado. Dylan actually offered me my first Account Executive position in Denver. Dylan would say to me every single day, "Leave no stone unturned. Sales is a numbers game." He inspired me to be different. Dylan taught me that the numbers were in my favor, it was just a matter of how I played the game.

This was a valuable lesson. I started walking into businesses simply asking questions. I would walk through the door of a business I had never seen before and march up to the front desk facing the evil "gatekeeper" and say, "Hi, my name is Michelle and I'm with Deep Rock Water here locally in Denver. Do you currently have a water system for your hard-working employees?"

Part of the power of "selling" is knowing your product(s). You can always ask questions, and you have to, to get to where you want to go with a conversation. However, it is much more powerful when you come to an objection, and you know without a doubt you can come back at them with a confident answer.

How many times are we told in sales to "look confident!" Well, how in the world am I supposed to look confident if I do not know much about anything. I like to think of this as TRIAL BY FIRE. Have you ever seen the cartoon where the little birdie gets kicked off the branch of the tallest tree you have ever seen, and you gasp because you know the birdie either must fly or die? That's how I have felt multiple times in sales! I guess I got used to this because I have learned that there is no faster way to learn than by failure, or "trial by fire."

Granted, most companies have training programs. Most of us don't get "thrown to the wolves" our first day. However, there is a time when you have to take a leap of faith and just get after it! Take those days and journal. Make notes of your successes and of your failures and as Mary Gaul would tell us, CELEBRATE!!!

SUCCESS!

Success is defined by our own thoughts.

My success may look 100% different than my "inspirations'" successes. In fact, that is an entirely different picture for each of us. We are different people with different values. They inspire me because they have shown me how to live life differently and to always look for the good.

Success should not define you. It is, however, an inner measurement of how you "feel" you are doing in life. Everyone likes to feel successful. Remember, it should not be a measure of your rank, or where you see yourself in life. It should simply level *you* up to *your own* expectations.

Beyond... (Living vs. Just Existing)

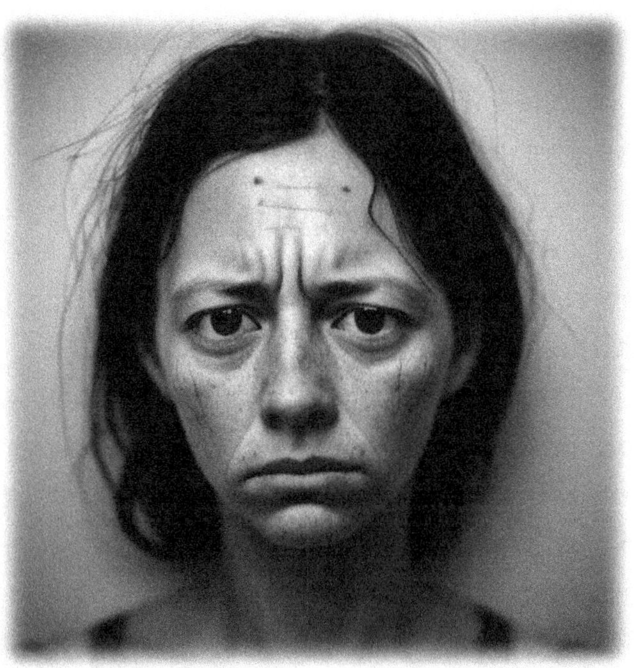

What is beyond success? Adventure!

The difference between living and just existing! This should be the number one goal in anyone's life. I want to always be in a place where I can LIVE vs. just exist.

I have had times in my life where I was "just existing."   I got in a funk and didn't know how to escape it. I was there recently. This is why mentors are so important in our lives.

To just exist is to roll through life living from paycheck to paycheck wondering how I'm going to pay the next bill. I never wanted this, but there I was. One accident that destroyed me, so I thought.

Unlucky or En Route To Destination Unknown

So, I have mentioned my accident...

I suppose I should share, to make this story make better sense to everyone. So here goes.

On December 16th, 2020, which was my 43rd birthday, I was in a horrible motor vehicle accident. My buddy, at the time, was driving me to the store near my house to pick up lunch, and we had intended to head right back to the house to hang out. We both were bankers for a local bank at the time. His birthday was on Friday, and mine was on Wednesday so we took a couple days off to celebrate both days.

On this dreadful day, we approached a stoplight. We waited at our red light as traffic flew by. Our light turned green. There was a vehicle across from us, so my buddy waited to go, to make sure the other vehicle was not going to turn in front of us.

The vehicle did not turn, so we started to go (remember this light has been green this entire time). I see, out of the corner of my eye, a gold flash to the right. I scream at the top of my lungs, "WATCH OUT!!!!" My buddy hit the brakes, and we started sliding. BAM, we were hit.

A gold van, out of nowhere, struck us going nearly 50 mph as she ran the red light at the intersection. The van hit the median and flew into the air, across four lanes of traffic, and landed backward on the sidewalk.

We sat in the Buick devastated. As my ears rang, I started to come back. Was I okay? I thought so. Oh, my goodness, what just happened! My glasses were now in the back seat. My phone that had been in my right pocket was now in the back seat. I tried to collect my thoughts and figure out if I was okay. My adrenaline was pumping so hard, I didn't know which way was up.

I looked at my friend and he was asking me if I was okay. I told him I thought so. I mean, I couldn't really tell. My arms and legs seemed to work, but my glasses were gone and my phone. Where was my phone? I needed to call for help! My friend went ahead and called 911.

He drove the car out of the intersection and we waited for the police to arrive. While we were waiting, my friend said he was going to go check on the lady who had hit us. I went with him.

We walked from our destroyed vehicle to the gold van. There was a witness asking the lady if she was okay. We looked inside the van and she was trapped inside. She was crying with a cell phone clenched in her hand, but mouthed that she was okay through the window.

We went back, after taking pictures, to our vehicle, and that is where I blacked out. I only remember two days later, when I was home on the couch recliner and I told my partner I couldn't move. I remember explaining that I felt like I had a major operation and that was the only way I knew how to explain it, was that it felt like after surgery the first time I had broken my neck.

To make a very long story short, I did have a broken neck (C3-C7) and back (L4, L5 and S1) and a Traumatic Brain Injury, and my pupils were knocked out of alignment. I guess I was "not okay."

Since this was not the intent of my book, I will keep this story to that, although there was much more to it. I want to stay on point: Sales.

Mission Not Yet Completed

There is so much more to my story that not many know, from being a Critical Care Paramedic, Firefighter and Rescue Diver, to working as a Behavioral Specialist, to just plain wanting to help others. My mission is not yet completed. Or, should I say, "My story isn't finished." (My newest bracelet from Jason).

That, is part of why I am writing this book. I've always loved to write. I am amid publishing another poetry anthology of some lighter poetry that is unique to me. It is called "A Touch of Me."

I'm not done. I want to live. I'm not going to sit here and "just exist" anymore. When you ask yourself at the start of your day, "Why?" Try to live. Not exist, but truly *LIVE*.

"JUST BE KIND" ...

63

"Always Be Humble & Kind"

This is all I have ever asked out of other humans in life. One simple thing...

"Just be kind."

Back To the Sale—Closure!

65

I've made a long story short. Or, is it that I have made a short story long?

I will leave that for you to decide. Regardless, I am hoping that I have made this a long lasting, never-ending, bunch of questions that gravitate in your mind. You will only get out of this what you put into it. I don't believe in reading something and then throwing it in the trash. I want this to be a "Guide." Your Guide to Success. This is clearly written for the beginner in sales, and one that is just learning the process of how Customer Relationship Management systems work. Most will quickly move past using Excel and into a more robust CRM program. This book was designed with simplicity and the newer sales mind at heart. It is a launch to help understand the methodologies behind how the CRMs were built and how they came around.

Please, take this for what you will. I do not claim to be the greatest success. I do not claim to know everything. I only know that these theories have worked in both my sales life and my everyday life. I want to share them with you, so that you may apply pieces that make sense for you, and that help you reach a level of success.

Remember, success, (not beauty, in this case--or is it?) is in the eye of the beholder. That, my friend, is *you*.

Go out there and create a success that makes you smile every single day when you wake up and look in the mirror. Let it be known what you do.

Success wasn't built based upon one person's philosophy. It's a conglomeration of ideas that have been tested over time. This is simply an addition to the history toward growing success. Use it wisely.

Now, go sell with passion and find the fire within you!

Client Relationship Management in Excel:

A User Guide

Welcome to your simplified Excel-based Client Relationship Management (CRM) system. Follow this guide to efficiently manage your client interactions, color-code them according to their engagement level, and utilize monthly tabs to track ongoing relationships.

SETTING UP THE CLIENT LIST

1. Open Excel and start a new workbook.
2. Name the first sheet as the current month (e.g., 'January').
3. Create column headers in Row 1:
   -A1: Client Full Name
   -B1: Complete Address
   -C1: Phone Number
   -D1: Notes

-E1: Status Color

4. Adjust column widths to ensure all information is visible.

ADDING CLIENTS

1. Enter client information in the corresponding rows under the headers.
2. Repeat for each new client.

COLOR CODING CLIENTS

1. Select a cell under 'Status Color' next to a client's details.
2. Go to the 'Home' tab, click 'Fill Color' (paint bucket icon) and choose the color corresponding to their status:
    -Blue: Company color, default for all new entries
    -Green: Client moving forward with a quote.

-Yellow: Follow-up in 6-12 months ('Call me later').

-Red: Not interested now ('Not now').

-Black: Do no contact again (Added to Do Not Call list). Blacking out eliminates future mistakes.

MONTHLY TABS AND CARRY-OVER

1. Create a new sheet for each month (click the "+" sign at the bottom tabs).
2. Name each new sheet accordingly (e.g., 'February', 'March', etc.).
3. Copy all non-black entries from the previous month to the new month.
   -Select the range with Green, Yellow, and Red Clients.
   -Right-click, choose 'Copy' or press 'Ctrl+C'.
   -Navigate to the new month's tab.
   -Right-click on the first cell in Row 2, choose 'Paste' or press 'Ctrl+V'.

4. Remove any unnecessary entries (those that have changed to Black).

UTILIZING FILTERS

1. Click the 'Data' tab, and select 'Filter' or use 'Ctrl+Shift+L' with the headers selected.
2. Filter icons appear in the header row.
3. Click the filter icon in the 'Status Color' column to sort or filter by color.
4. Choose a color to view only clients with that status.

ADDITIONAL DETAILS (FOR ADVANCED USERS)

As you become more accustomed to the CRM, you can add columns for:

-Email Address
-Last Contact Date
-Next Contact Due
-Salesperson Assigned

You can also incorporate conditional formatting to automatically color-code based on status inputted, use more nuanced categorizing, and integrate formulas to calculate days until next follow-up.

SAVING AND BACKUP

-Save your workbook regularly (press 'Ctrl+S').
-Create backups by saving copies in different locations (cloud storage, external hard drives, etc.).

Remember, this Excel-based CRM is flexible; feel free to tweak it to suit your specific needs. Happy managing!

Acknowledgements

I would like to take a moment to thank everyone who has helped me make this possible.

I want to thank my partner in life, Chenae Carroll. She has supported me through life's most challenging battles and continues to do so. She has cared for me when I have been down. And, I have been down more than most, so to her, I am forever grateful.

MaryAnn Bostron Lucero, a wonderful friend and technical writer, was kind enough to be my editor. MaryAnn has been in my life for around 10 years now. She is very important to me. It was an honor to have her partake in my journey.

I also want to shout out to all of my friends who have put up with me through my crazy times. My best friend through college went through a terrible time as I was writing this. John, I want you to know, I love you forever. John has since passed.

Jason has been my best friend and my rock through these last two major battles. Jason has his own story. He's a survivor. He will forever be my best friend. Why? Because he cares. No matter what. He always cares.

The whole point of this book was about caring and the why behind what I do. I could go on for hours about people I want to thank, but I won't because I am grateful for everyone in my life. Just know that if you have ever known me, there was a reason we met.

My mom always told me that everything happens for a reason. So, for her, I believe.

NOTES

About the Author

Michelle I Wolford is an outgoing adventure seeker who hails from Lewellen, Nebraska. With a passion for the great outdoors, she loves to fish, hunt, and golf in her free time. Growing up, Michelle discovered her athletic talents and became a State Champion Triple Jumper in Track & Field.

Michelle's media presence is also noteworthy, having appeared on television twice. She made appearances on ESPN and KNOP TV, showcasing her skills and sharing her experiences. Additionally, Michelle had the opportunity to be on air on iHeart Radio, further expanding her reach.

In her pursuit of adventure, Michelle is often drawn to lakes and golf courses, where she finds solace and enjoyment. She embodies an energetic spirit and a love for the outdoors that continues to drive her passions and create memorable experiences.